C LINT BALLINGER BEGAN HIS interest in economic development in the very long run while at The University of Texas at Austin. While there he worked with the World's oldest accounting tokens (Mesopotamian, 8000-3500 BC) under Denise Schmandt-Besserat and researched the development of both State and credit-money with a special interest in the debt-deflation work of Irving Fisher. For his M.A. in Political Science at The University of North Carolina at Chapel Hill he focused on modern uneven economic development, and went on to specialize in the interpretation of global econometric data for his PhD in Geography at Cambridge University.

How Your Professor Should Have Explained
The Principles of Macroeconomics
But Didn't

I T TOOK OVER 9,000 YEARS from the earliest human settlements to the dawning of modern states and modern banking systems circa 1500 AD.

It took several more centuries for the gradual appearance of reasonably accurate albeit sporadic descriptions of the role of states and banks in the creation of currencies and their profound roles of capital development and social coordination in both the public and private spheres.

This progress was briefly interrupted by an intellectual decline of Economics into a period of real-world irrelevance (~1950~2008). However, led by a handful of pioneering economists, and not yet in classrooms or textbooks, earlier partial theories of the two coordinating systems of the macroeconomy were revived in the 1990s and then, more crucially, consolidated into a unified understanding of how real-world economies actually function. Economic understanding emerged into a Golden Age of which the present generation is in the exciting midst of.

1000 Castaways compresses this 10,000 years of economic development into several years and a society small enough to allow an illuminating overview, yet large enough to feature the institutions essential to modern economies. Centuries of economic thought are distilled for the reader to the essence of how the macroeconomy functions (and malfunctions).

A RENEGADE BAND OF Modern Monetary Theorists has overturned mainstream economics in part by emphasizing that there is not one, but two systems of modern money, the "vertical" and the "horizontal." They conclusively demonstrate how unifying our understanding of these is crucial for grasping modern economics.

"the key to understanding Modern Monetary Theory is this vertical-horizontal relationship" (Warren Mosler)

1000 Castaways develops Mosler's statement into a concise, book-length treatment that is accessible to all readers, starting from first principles and, step-by-step, leading the reader up to the complexities of the real world.

Our one thousand castaways develop, before our eyes, a "perfect" economy, and demonstrate how the horizontal and vertical systems of money naturally emerge from even more fundamental organizational needs of a large society.

1000 Castaways then contrasts the Island's "economics" with real-world "economics," in an enlightening illustration of the last few steps in our common economic understanding that we must take in order to run our modern economies in a way that maximizes wellbeing.

cjballinger@gmail.com

ISBN 978-0-6483906-1-9
eBook ISBN 9780648390602

aetiology /ˌiːtɪˈɒlədʒi/, noun, (Oxford English Dictionary, def. 2): the investigation or attribution of the cause or reason for something, often expressed in terms of historical or mythical explanation.

ÆEtiology

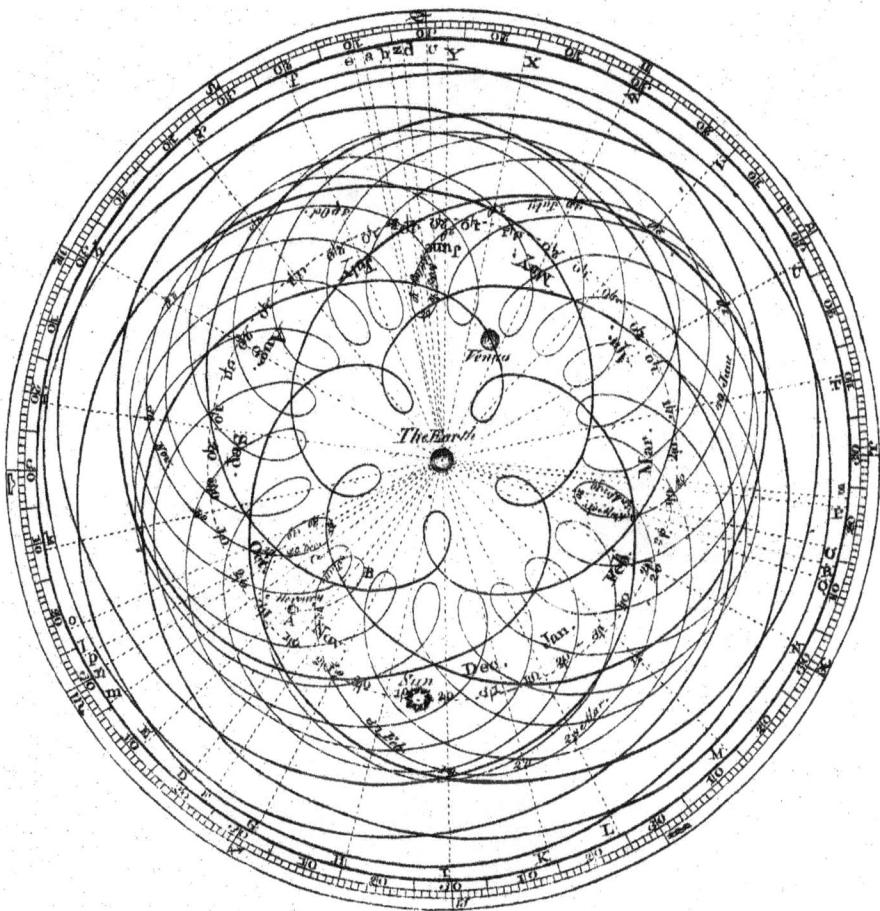

1000 CASTAWAYS

FUNDAMENTALS
of
ECONOMICS

Clint Ballinger

Æstidgy

Contents

From ancient times there emerged two systems for coordinating the optimal use of real resources in an economy

One coordinates the private use of factors of production

Another coordinates group decisions to carry out group projects

And one unit binds them all

Understanding these two systems and their interaction underlies all further understanding of the macroeconomy

INTRODUCTION

O VER THE BROAD SWEEP of history economic well-being has primarily increased because of advances in technology and human organization. Understanding the latter is the key to understanding the macroeconomy and is the topic of this book.

Before imagining our group of a thousand castaways, imagine an island of just ten people. You are on a sailboat, along with nine others, that crashes onto a small deserted island. You have a pretty good idea you won't be discovered for a very long time, months or perhaps years. So you go about first trying to survive, and then trying to thrive: to improve your long-term material well-being as much as possible.

The ten of you do what you can to get the necessities of life—to build shelter and provide food and water. You each have your own interests and abilities and work on small personal projects such as making fishing nets or cutting and carving posts to build huts and so on.

On these individual projects it nevertheless often makes sense to enlist the help of one or several of the others. For example, it takes two people to drag a net through the shallow lagoon effectively, and several people working together can harvest coconut groves more efficiently than one person climbing and collecting alone.

In addition to several castaways working together on these individual projects, the ten of you sometimes decide to all work together to build something for the whole group. The whole group might decide that it makes sense to dig a deep well together, or to build a path into the center of the island to drag timber and sleds of fruit out of the forest.

The ten castaways thus have two primary "macroeconomic" problems to solve. The first is to maximize the productivity of their private projects. The second is how to arrange the group projects they sometimes want to carry out together. In addition to resolving these two primary issues, your small group will want to make sure that, combined, your projects are using your resources effectively. For example, you won't want a field of ripe fruit to go unharvested because you didn't make a trail into the woods, or a lagoon full of fish to swim away because no one was available to fish or you hadn't built good nets to catch them.

With only ten people everyone knows each other well, and both small individual projects and larger group projects are easily arranged. Everyone knows each other personally, can trust that small favors and gifts will be reciprocated, and the benefit from coordination and the fair distribution of the resulting goods is clearly visible in most cases.

However, as the size of a group goes up, trust, personal knowledge of each other, and communication across the whole group rapidly becomes more difficult. You have to work with people you do not know, people who don't trust each other, and group projects, even if popularly decided on, are hard to organize. At one hundred people basic communication is difficult. At millions, whole new methods of organization must emerge for a group to be prosperous.

This book looks at a society small enough for us to easily maintain a birds-eye (macro) view of it, but just large enough for the group to require the key institutions our modern society of millions needs to function well. These are our 1,000 Castaways.

Despite consisting of countries with millions of people, in our modern society the two primary macroeconomic challenges above were met by the emergence of two fundamental systems that are crucial to guiding the economy. Understanding these two systems, how they are used, and how they interact, is the key story we need to know for a true understanding of the macroeconomy of all large democratic societies.

This book tells that story.

Part I

THE ISLAND

CHAPTER 1

THE ISLAND: SYSTEM ONE (HORIZONTAL)

A FLEET OF A THOUSAND COLONISTS are blown off course for weeks by a series of violent cyclones, eventually crashing onto the reefs of a large uncharted island. All of their ships and provisions are lost to sea. They wash ashore, all surviving the stormy night. As morning breaks they begin their search for water and possible food sources.

The survivors struggle in this foreign land at first. They

collect crabs at the rocky tideline, forage along the dense forest-edge, and weave simple palm leaf baskets to collect the many unidentifiable fruits they find in the forest.

As time passes they begin to be more successful at fishing, and also manage to get some shoots of wild yam-like tubers to sprout in small raised-mound gardens. Eventually they begin to have enough food and also begin to build larger, sturdier, more permanent shelters.

In time they have enough goods to live in relative comfort and began to produce more of what they each specialize in than they need to survive. They do this in order to trade the products they specialize in for other things they need or want. A fisher catches an extra basket of fish, for example, to trade for someone else's extra yams. This way both of them end up with more variation than they might otherwise.

However, sometimes a trade is not easy. For example, if one villager catches a very large amount of fish and wants some yams instead of all the fish, he may not be able to find someone who has extra yams who also wants fish. This is especially a problem as he can't even save the fish and hope in a few days to find a willing trader since fish go off quickly. And the problem of finding a "double coincidence of wants" is even more complex because he might actually want many different things, like some yams but also a few coconuts, some cord someone has spun, and maybe an offer to pay some fish to have a skilled builder help with his hut. It would be very difficult to try to chase down willing traders for all of these different products.

Meanwhile, the Islanders have discovered wild barley and began cultivating it. It is useful to make bread and por-ridge, but is especially valued for easily making quality beer.

Bags of wild barley begin to be traded around as it is easy to divide into smaller portions, is highly valued, and stores well. Soon they realize that they can trade their main product (fish or yams or anything else) that they have a surplus of for barley bags. Since the grain keeps, is easily dividable, and everyone likes barley products across the whole island, it is then easy to trade small bags of barley for all the little things they wanted above. The burlap bags of barley also don't rot quickly like fish, so they can wait a few days (or much more) until the builder is free or the yams have been harvested to trade them. The bags of barley work as a "middleman" item for the islanders. It is a commodity that can easily be traded, a simple "commodity money."[1]

THE ISLANDERS ARE WORKING hard to survive but are always aware that they could increase their production if they could organize their resources and labor better. For example, one Islander, John, has been fishing with a small net he made. He could, however, catch 10 times as many fish with a really large, well-woven net. But he would need a lot

[1] This story of commodity trade leading to something "money-like" corresponds to what happened over extremely long time periods with grain trade in the Ancient Near East, between emerging social groups, governments, and individuals (as we will see, it developed as somewhat of a "hybrid" of what I name here System One and System Two; it took thousands of years for early "proto-money" systems to fully evolve into the two distinct systems discussed here; Ch. 5 discusses this further). Modern anthropological studies of smaller-scale, simpler societies show that they do not develop barter systems in this way. Some (Graeber 2011, see Strauss 2016 for a good summary) have concluded from this that commodity barter did not pre-date "money" at all (in part as an appropriate backlash against overly "market" oriented economics) [cont...]

of help and material to build such a net and he is too busy just getting by to save the resources to build it. If John worked slowly on such a net himself it would take him many months to weave it. In the meantime the whole island is suffering from having fewer fish than they could have if John had a bigger net.[2]

John decides to promise his friends and neighbors that if they help him make a lot of rope and weave a large net now he will pay them from the many extra fish he is going to catch in the future. They all pitch in and a

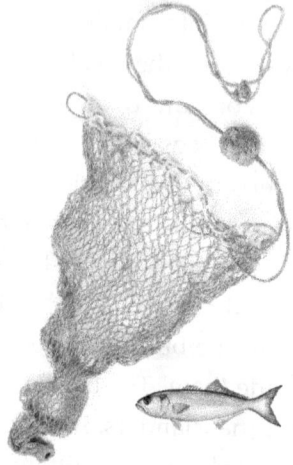

However, they are confusing both time scales and size scales. The barter account is an accurate simplified account of what happened over very long time periods a very long time ago among a particular set of the "civilizing" (first "city-developing") cultures in a particular place, the Ancient Near East (and again, inextricably entwined with credit and government "money" systems). It is incorrect to conclude barter commodity-trade did not happen at all, and very early in human prehistory, based on smaller, modern tribes and groups. Barley did indeed develop into a money-like unit of account for barter in the Ancient Near East, regardless of what happens in "less developed" modern small groups and tribes.

2 John is creating "capital," which is anything we create that helps us create other things. For example, a loom that helps us make cloth faster is capital. A spinning wheel that helps us make pottery faster is capital. When the capital goods we use for production are owned primarily by individuals and private companies the resulting system is generally called "capitalism." In practice many goods, such as those involving networks, are more efficiently produced by group ownership; these issues are discussed later..

large effective net is soon made. We can see how this small group of friends, simply by organizing themselves, has increased their ability to produce and thus made themselves all materially better off.

This way of increasing production worked for John because his friends and neighbors knew and trusted him and they could work out the repayment method easily. However, with even a small increase in scale this type of agreement begins to be hard to achieve, since people do not trust strangers (either to do what they said or to be skillful enough) and it becomes difficult to agree to details of payment.

One way these problems of knowledge and trust in larger groups can be overcome is by formally writing out agreements and having them executed by someone the community trusts and who is capable of honoring the agreements.

This is best illustrated by a further example. Imagine the same scenario but John lives among a much larger group. There is a group of prosperous farmers (we'll call them the "Farmers Group") who have found it beneficial to arrange small projects like John's fishing net with many people in their community. They know John and that he has proven trustworthy on other small projects in the past.

John does not have many friends who can help with his nets, but instead asks a group of workers he sees in town. They hesitantly agree. But how will John pay them? He doesn't have barley (or fish) now and they have no way to trust him.

John asks the Farmers Group to write notes promising to pay agreed-upon weights of barley on John's behalf if the workers will help with the nets. The Farmers Group writes the agreements down on their ledgers.

The workers know the Farmers Group is wealthy enough and trustworthy enough to be able and willing to pay them. The Farmers Group knows that if the project is successful they will all be better off, and also of course take a cut of the deal for themselves.

The "promises to pay" by the farmers are enough to get the strangers to help John. The larger nets are made, more fish are caught, and everyone is better off on the Island. The Farmers Group honors the ledger promises to pay the workers on John's behalf, and John over time pays the farmers group back.

The key thing that has happened is that the existence of the Farmers Group and their "promises-to-pay" have allowed even a group of strangers in a large society to cooperate and to get better nets built and increase the real resources of the Island. They have converted trust and organization into real, physical goods.

This system works well, and over time people realize that they can transfer these ledger entries like bags of barley. (In the real world this process occurred extremely gradually and with countless setbacks, over not even centuries but rather over many millennia).

A Monumental Step: Transferability

THE BIGGEST STEP TO making IOUs into "money" is making them transferable (also called being "negotiable"). This is not easy in a large society as there is no obvious way for a stranger to trust not only you, but to trust what you are claiming to be a valid IOU from someone else is indeed valid.

Imagine the scenario above again. One of the workers, Heidi, is helping John weave his nets. John "paid" her by having the Farmers Group write a promise-to-pay entry in their ledger, just like he paid the workers he met in town who are helping him.

Heidi has work on her house she wants done. But she also (like John) doesn't have any extra bags of barley to pay someone to help her. But she does have the ledger entry from John. She knows the carpenter she wants to do the work, so she asks him if he will accept the ledger entry for payment.

The carpenter knows the Farmer Group always pays its promises (if someone has a ledger entry and asks to redeem it for bags of barley they can and will), so he accepts Heidi's offer. He does the work and she transfers the ledger entry (instead of barley) to the carpenter. The carpenter can redeem the ledger entry by having the farmers honor their promises and change it for barley, or he can save it on the ledger and exchange it for goods or services like Heidi did.

In this way ledger entries (and similarly, "promissory notes" circulating as paper, functioning in the same way) eventually became the money of a region (as we mentioned, in the real world this process took many thousands of years to fully evolve). Individuals and businesses used a trusted, financially sound group (like the Farmers Group) to create promises-to-pay. Today, of course, we call these "banks."

The key role the banks carry out that allows for IOUs to become "money" is to be a trusted middleman. Note, however, that although this is a common understanding of the key role banks play, the point of this chapter is to explain why the role of banks in getting capital-increasing projects off the ground is far more important. It is this property that dramatically raises the material wellbeing of societies, more even than the monumental step of banks in allowing IOUs to be transferred.

This whole system, then, emerges somewhat naturally to create a monetary system for the Island. It uses bags of barley as its unit of account, but is actually made up of "promises to pay" in this unit, not barley itself. In other words, you could buy something with a standard weight of barley, but most people are also willing to sell their goods and services in exchange for the "promises to pay" ledger entries by the Farmers Group or similar institutions across the Island. They generally find the ledger entries more convenient, so this over time becomes the dominant way of transacting.

The crucial aspect of this system, however, is not that it creates a money system. Much more importantly, it is that this system "monetizes creditworthiness" and thus allows for projects that raise productivity to be carried out. It allows for projects like John's nets, but tens of thousands of times over, to occur on the Island. Projects that otherwise would not get done. This greatly increases the material wellbeing (the variety, quality, and amount of consumer goods) of the whole Island many times over what it would be without this system of trust.

The material wealth that societies with well-developed systems like the one described above is far greater than those with less developed systems of trust.[3] The banking system is only a little about creating a private monetary system. *The far more important role it carries out is allowing for the organization of private productive enterprise on scales unimaginable in societies without such systems.* This makes the material wellbeing of society many times greater, providing many times more material goods such as food, clothing, entertainment, and services.

Important Points To Remember For Future Chapters:

Loanable funds

It is important to emphasize that this type of "money" is created by banks making IOUs *denominated* in something, but not actually *lending out* that something. Why is this important? Because it means that they do not sit around and wait to have that something deposited to them before they lend again.

Similarly, modern banks do not wait around for deposits

---

3 This system of credit was not really perfected until the mid-2nd Millennium in western Eurasia, from about 1500 AD. That is, exactly when that part of the world had a meteoric rise in prosperity and power. For a modern example, the Soviet Union demonstrates the power of this system (through its absence). There have been many theories as to why the Soviet Union collapsed. However, often unremarked is that one of the primary differences between the Soviet Union and the "West" was that the Soviet Union did not have a private banking system, a "Farmers Group." What kind of production might a society have if they do not have funding for private production using capital goods? If people like John had to continue fishing only with their small original net? The primary complaints of people in the Soviet Union regarding their quality of life revolved around the quantity and quality of goods that were common in the "West." It is easy to imagine how this this affected the long-term viability, including military viability, of the Soviet Union.

of dollars, or pounds, or yen. They also simply create, out of thin air, accounting entries in their customers' accounts, who can then spend them. These accounting entries are not actual dollars or pounds or yen, but promises to pay those on your behalf. Understanding that banks do not wait around for "loanable funds" to be deposited has profound effects on the way an economy works, something we discuss later.

"Money" creation and inflation

Note that System One is not necessarily inflationary from "money" creation for two reasons:

1. In System One, every loan that creates credit-money also creates a debt. The system as a whole always nets to zero. Accounting for all positive account balances and debts in the economy = zero.

2. Because System One increases production along with the expansion of balance sheets. There is more credit money, but there are more things to spend it on.

The only way this system can contribute to inflation is if it exceeds "2" above. That is, if it begins giving loans for non-productive enterprises, in other words, creating more credit-money without a corresponding increase in productivity. This has two effects : a) causing inflation especially in the type of business the loans are made for (especially notable in real estate and higher education) and b) the bloated system puts unearned "promises to pay" in the pockets of finance, real estate, insurance and related industries. These become real claims on real resources. In other words, a corrupt system enriches those involved in it at everyone else's expense. Just "netting to zero" is not enough - the private system has to be the right size for the economy, and no bigger.

Balance Sheet Expansion

Note that, for a bank, adding a number into a customer's account for credits and onto their own as a liability (debt) is what it known as a balance sheet expansion. As a bank makes more loans it is liable to pay on more people's behalf. It has grown its balance sheet. For example, the agreement between John and the Farmers Group can be thought of like this:

Assets	Liabilities
+500	-500
Promise from John to the Farmers Group to repay 500 barley units (earned from his future fishing success)	Promise by the Farmers Group *to pay on John's behalf* barley units, up to 500 units (to those helping John make nets now)

This would be simplified to look like this on the Farmers Group balance sheet/ledger (no - or + sign are needed as assets and liabilities already signify the sign):

Assets	Liabilities
500	500

Combining the balance sheet expansions of all banks is the sum total of the credit- money system. Both sides grow and shrink as much as the economy needs, with the total always netting to zero.

Other systems of finance besides System One

This trust related system is one of the most powerful developments for increasing private production of consumer goods. However, important to later discussion, there are three other ways that a process like John's fishing nets can be achieved. The first is of course System One. The second, third and fourth methods are:

2. In a society still using a commodity money, a person or group could save that real money and actually loan/invest it with interest. So John would directly borrow a commodity money (in this scenario, barley) to pay his workers and if profitable, pay it back to lenders (those who saved it). In other words, in this case, the transactions would be like most people imagine banks to be - someone actually saving deposits before loaning them out or investing them. This contrasts with the Farmers Group and normal modern banks, which do not wait for deposits, but rather operate on "promises to pay," and create these out of thin air for creditworthy borrowers. The existence of the latter does not preclude people actually saving first to lend or invest, although the credit system is much much more significant in the real world now.

3. Similarly, John could issue ownership in his project. So John would form a company and sell "stock" in it. The funds from selling the stock would fund employing

help to make nets, while the holders of the stock would be paid from the profits as part owners.

4. Similarly, John could borrow by selling bonds. These are like stocks but rather than ownership in his project, would just be promises to pay some fixed return, at which point the bonds mature and are no longer an obligation to John. Note John or a company probably could not do this if they were in John's earlier position of most people not knowing if they could trust him or his project. In other words, if John had that trust he could bypass the Farmers Group (Bank) but without that trust he needs the Farmers Group.

The primary system for increasing private production that we will discuss, however, is System One.

The product of System One, the "promises to pay" ledger entries or paper notes eventually spread throughout the Island. However, as we are about to see...something else was happening at the same time (Chapter 2).

System one creates what is known as "horizontal" or "inside" money

This type of "money" from System One in our real world is known as bank credit-money, "horizontal money" or "inside money."

Some version of the story I told above is used to explain the emergence of horizontal money. The way horizontal money functions is generally not understood by the general public (nor many economists, especially prior to 2008). However, often it is the end product of this fascinating process—the horizontal money system itself—that is held up as the most important part of the story. As we will see, it is not. System One itself is, as we shall see, what is important, not horizontal money *per se*.

Interest

An important note to remember for future chapters: With a commodity money, such as bags of barley or gold, if one saves, it of course earns no interest. Similarly, saved "promises to pay" do not earn interest.

The only way to earn a return on saved "money" is to invest it in a productive enterprise such as John's. This concept has been understood since at least Roman times, where if you wanted interest on money deposited with Roman bankers *(argentarius)*, they would invest or loan that money, putting it both at real risk and genuinely out of hand. If you only wanted them to safely hold the money for you, it was called *vacua pecunia*, "empty money," and earned zero interest. Neither a saved commodity nor a saved "promise to pay" naturally earns interest. Interest or some return on "money" comes from investing it, not saving or hoarding it.

CHAPTER 2

THE ISLAND:
SYSTEM TWO
(VERTICAL)

S O FAR, IN THE first chapter, we have seen how a
system can emerge naturally that functions to help
individuals better coordinate the use of real
resources and thus increase the private production of society
overall. This increases the production of real goods and services for everyone. The "money" system ("promises-to-pay"
system) this creates is very useful in itself. But of more fundamental importance is the role of this system in helping
coordinate the private sector's use of resources in a way that

can increase the material wellbeing of the whole group.

Some projects, however, are much larger or longer-term than John's fishing nets, much too large for any one person or even group of people to want to engage in. And some projects are less obviously profitable to any one person but still desired by the group as a whole, especially as they often increase, sometimes by many times, the productivity of the private sector.

For example, the Islanders desired a road across the middle of the island to speed up trade in timber and stone (a public project greatly increasing the quality and amount of housing they can build on their own), but this was far too big a project for any one person or small group to do together. They also wanted a system to take care of the kids on the island and teach them useful things while the parents were making nets and farming yams and barley in the day. Both of these projects can raise the wellbeing of the Islanders, especially in the long run.

They think about trying to organize and coordinate everyone to do certain tasks: appoint road-builders and rock quarriers and teachers and book writers and so on. But this would be a monumentally complicated task. However, they know that if they do not build the road, or schools, and similar projects in the group's interest, their long-term wellbeing and private productivity will be much less than it would be if these public projects are done.

ONE EVENING, AT THEIR weekly fireside meeting held around a smoldering red fire under the stars, a wizened old woman tells a story she read long ago in a dusty leatherbound book. The ancients had faced a similar problem, she explains. They wanted grand projects done—Pyramids for their Gods and grand irrigation projects to grow grain to feed their military. So they gathered their useless scrap metal and made up small, worthless tokens but stamped their images on them. They decreed that 1,000 of these cheap tokens would be demanded of every adult every year on pain of death. The only way to obtain these tokens was to work on the grand public projects, where workers would be paid in these same tokens.

This meant that every adult had to work for the public projects in order to be able to pay the tribute demanded by the rulers at the end of the year. The rulers could enforce this because they had the monopoly on power in that region. In other words, in that territory no one could force the rulers to do anything but the rulers could use any amount of force they wanted or needed to make others do things. This is the defining property of sovereignty—a monopoly on force over a region.

This system had the effect of moving, from the private sector, all of the labor and resources needed for the ruler's grand pyramids and irrigation projects.

"There was an interesting side effect of all of this" the wizened old woman declares, firelight flashing in her eyes. "The tokens, despite being made of worthless scrap and not bags of barley or gold or silver, became valued by all to pay their yearly tribute, and soon could be used to buy anything in the society, just like bags of barley or gold."

The tokens, in other words, had become "money." Even though they were made of worthless scrap metal rather than a commodity metal, they were highly valued by everyone for everything because of the general demand for them to pay back the yearly tribute the rulers demanded.[4]

T HE WIZENED OLD WOMAN looked around at the red firelight playing on the faces of the others. She could see worried thoughts on their faces, imagining themselves toiling away on useless pyramids and vast mounded-earth dams. She quickly pointed out that even though sometimes this token system was done purely for tribute and selfish reasons by the ancient rulers, it could also be done simply to co-ordinate the provision of things the group wants but can't coordinate privately. In other words, instead of acting like Egyptian Pharaohs, they could use the token system as a fair and efficient way to move some of their private effort towards making the public goods they need like the road and the schools. In a democracy it can actually serve as a volun-

---

4 Throughout history coins often functioned in this way, their value due their ability to pay tribute, fines, and/or taxes, rather than their precious metal content. This was often not fully understood, so a complex mix of coins made with precious metals (having ingot value) and value as a tax unit endured for millennia. In retrospect, one of the chief benefits to rulers from using precious metals was not that this gave value to the coin as a commodity. The benefit was that it made counterfeiting the coin virtually impossible for the general public. This of course was especially important before (centuries) later anti-counterfeiting methods from printing (and now still more sophisticated methods) were developed.

tary, *market* solution to coordinating all the complex projects the group itself wants.

For example, the Islanders might decide among themselves that they want to build themselves a road and a school. Each Islander would promise, say, 100 hours towards the project. They would get a ledger entry for each hour they contribute among themselves. At the end of the year they prove their contribution.

Like the ledger entries for John's fishing nets, these ledger entries become valued in themselves. Imagine Heidi, who wanted a carpenter to work on her home, has contributed 80 hours to the group's projects. Rather than pay the carpenter with promises-to-pay from the farmers group, she might tell him she will transfer him ten ledger entries if he works on her home. He agrees and does the work. In fact, he may decide to do this ten times over. This allows him to pay his 100 units at the end of the year, while other people will have worked the hours towards the group project for him, and Heidi got work from the carpenter done.

They decide to call these units "crusoes." They can be used to pay the obligation the group demands to get public works done, and one crusoe is one tax-credit.

T HERE ARE TWO REASONS to carry out group projects. The first is that they are projects that although the group as a whole benefits from and want, would in fact not get done by the private system. This includes roads and basic infrastructure, education, caring for the sick and elderly, "pure" research, and maintaining common areas such as parks.

Although the private system is good for creating more consumer goods, for example, even if it expanded greatly it would not likely reach the potential and mix of goods the society could reach with both private and public projects. In other words, no matter how much the private system grows, it would not always supply the kinds of projects that the Islanders want and that increases their overall wellbeing.

Additionally, there is a very substantial amplifying of private production from public projects. For example, a public bridge might vastly increase the amount of goods that private farmers and merchants can get to market. The public project amplifies the amount of private goods, and raises the overall material wellbeing of society over what the private system alone would achieve. In the longer-term, public education and public health increase the productivity of the Island. Investment in public projects, especially with goods and labor that might not have been utilized by private production, can, in time, amplify the overall goods of a society many times over. We will discuss the merits of public projects further in Chapter 3.

The Final Step: Unifying The Two Systems

E VENTUALLY, BECAUSE BOTH SYSTEMS are really just ledger entries (or paper notes), and barley is a commodity (or gold or any other commodity if it were being used in an early society) like any other, the idea is hit on to replace the "promise to pay" in the bank-credit system from bags of barley to crusoes, the "tax-credit" of the Island.

[Note, this could and at times surely did happen in reverse: A tribute "unit" with value because it is demanded by the government for fines and taxes could then develop into the unit of

account of a nascent private system; this book is not about the historical development of money and banking per se and I am purposefully moving on to a fully-developed system as quickly as possible. The two possibilities actually probably both happened many times, with thousands of different permutations, across hundreds of cultures and thousands of years.]

Imagine John and his fishing nets. In Chapter One, the Farmers Group monetized his creditworthiness by creating a ledger entry that he could use to pay workers to help him. There has to be some unit of account for everyone to agree on, even if that unit (bags of barley in that case) is not actually used at all.

But now that tax-credits—"crusoes"—have been created on the Island and their value is accepted across the Island, they can replace weights of barley as a unit of account. So if John now goes to a bank (like the Farmers Group), the bank will create a ledger entry (loan) to him, but now it will be measured in crusoes, not barley. Anyone who has an entry created for them in a private ledger could redeem that promise at any time by having the "bank" pay your tax obligation.

So both System One and System Two now share the same unit of account, the crusoe. In the real world, this is how all modern economies function. Their unit of account, the Dollar, Pound, Yen, Swiss Franc, Krone, Peso, Naira, Rupee and so on, is the "tax-credit" of that corresponding country.

Creating a single currency that is shared by both the private and public systems is efficient and useful. However, focusing on this aspect, although highly interesting, masks something far more important.

It seems to us, the modern users of the currency, that there is only one system, as a dollar or pound or yen paid to us by the government (if we work for them or have a contract with the government) and a "promise to pay" dollar transferred to our bank account from another bank all work the same for us.

In fact, however, the two parts of the system continue to operate in very different ways, and, more importantly, contribute to our wellbeing in two very distinct ways. Even in our modern economies with modern unified currencies, System One and System Two perform distinct roles and raise overall material wellbeing in their distinct ways.

As we will see—highlighting the fact that our single currency actually arises from two ancient and very different systems that still exist to this day is the key to understanding our modern economy and raising our wellbeing.

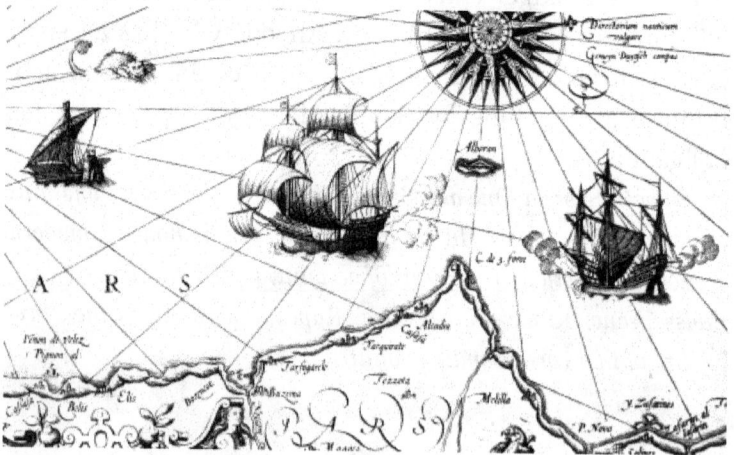

A Few Things To Remember Before Moving On...

Electronic money/accounting entries

Note that on the Island the two systems are "running" on ledgers. This will allow us to bring the Island up to a modern-type economy more easily; our real world now runs almost entirely on electronic ledgers. We can imagine that some of the ledger entries are allowed to be passed around as notes, so the Islanders have paper money as well, but the ledger system for banks and for the group is dominant as it is in our modern world now.

(Historically, and in existence in Hong Kong, for example, real "promissory bank notes" circulated, credit-notes from System One issued by banks. However, in most modern countries governments only allows notes from System Two (made by the government and being official government tax-credits) to be passed around as bills or notes. In other words, if you take cash out of your bank, the bank is in effect redeeming your claim for "real" government (System Two) "money.")

Access to System Two "Money" (tax-credits)

Also note that although the Islanders can transact in System Two "money" as cash, they can also directly transact and save tax-credits (crusoes) *on the main tax-credit ledger of the Island.*

In our modern systems citizens do *not* have access to ledger (nor electronic ledger) entries of their saved tax-credits. You do not have an account with US Dollars in it at Wells Fargo—you only have a ledger entry by Wells Fargo *promising to pay* some amount of real US Dollars on your behalf.

In the real world citizens can neither directly transact in tax-credits ($, £, ¥, ₩, ฿, ₼, ₦, ₪, etc.) nor directly save them. They always must run their transactions and savings through banks as System One "promises to pay." They can, as we will see, *convert* their saved "promises to pay" held by a bank into another type of government token, what we call "bonds" (or "securities"; also "treasuries" in the US, "gilts" in the UK. The most common general term is "bonds").

We will discuss the reasons for and significance of these arrangements in Chapter 5: The Real World.

Direct spending of tax-credits (crusoes) into the economy

Also note that the group of Islanders spend the government currency they have created (crusoes, which are tax-credits) *directly* into the economy. The process in the real world is usually much more complex. We will also explore the reason for this and its significance in Chapter 5: The Real World.

Chapter 3

Balancing the Two Systems

I N THE INTRODUCTION WE discussed how, in order to maximize their material wellbeing, a small group of people would want both to organize their private activities and their group activities efficiently. This is relatively easy with ten people but becomes exponentially harder as a group scales up in size.

Two different systems emerged to overcome the difficulty of scaling-up private and group coordination and make modern economies. The horizontal (credit-money) system serves to allow the Islanders to coordinate their private activities more efficiently. The vertical (government tax-credit; "crusoes" on the Island) system both allows public projects to be coordinated more efficiently and these in turn also amplify the productivity of the private system.

A third goal, directly related to the two systems above, would be to make sure that the group are not wasting available resources, reducing everyone's wellbeing below what it could be. Let's consider this third point in greater detail.

It is obvious that using all of one's desired resources efficiently provides greater prosperity than letting some useful resources go to waste. Imagine again the little ten-person island from the Introduction. It has a certain amount of resources—the abilities and labor of the ten castaways plus potable water, coconut trees, fish, and so on. Think of all these resources as being inside this box:

Now imagine that everything the islanders actually use and do is represented by this box:

If the amount the islanders use and do is less than all

their desired possible resources, then the gray box would be smaller than the block box. We can picture this like this:

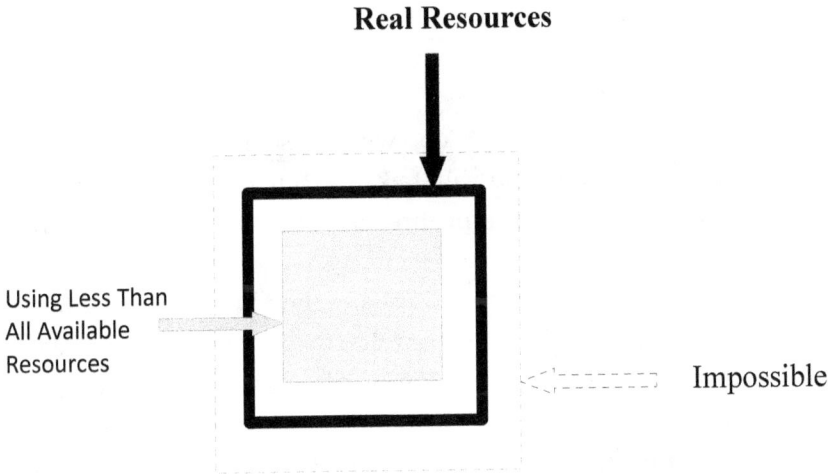

Real Resources

Using Less Than
All Available
Resources

Impossible

The ideal economy of the ten people would be to have all their activity fill the black box. This would raise their wellbeing to the highest it could potentially be given the resources and technology that they have. This same concept holds true for larger economies such as the 1000 Castaways' Island and those in our real world as well.

Unemployment And Spinning Cord

IMAGINE THE TEN CASTAWAYS begin to specialize some. Three of them are especially good at deep-sea fishing from one of their only small rafts. But sometimes for days on end storm swells and strong currents make deep-sea fishing impossible. Also suppose that two of the castaways suffer from occasional bouts of allergies that make them unable to do their usual valued tasks of tending the plots of yams they manage to grow for everyone.

The usual "economy" of the island is everyone doing their "private sector" job, with these five specializing in deep-sea fishing and yam farming. But sometimes there is a downturn where two or three or even five of the castaways are unable to do their usual job.

However, there are always a million little tasks that need to get done on the island but that they never seem to be able to find the time to do. For example, they can never seem to find enough time to weave all the seemingly endless palm mats they need for roofs that leak, floors in their huts, cooking with, eating on, storing food with, and so on. They also make cord and rope for all their nets and fishing and tying bamboo poles together for huts. They make the cord by spinning coconut-husk fibers together. This is also used for fishing nets and line, traps, tying roof mats down on huts, hammocks etc. They are literally always behind on weaving and spinning cord and rope.

The best "economy" for the food production and living standards of the group is when the two castaways with allergies are able to farm and the weather conditions allow the three fishers to fish. But in a downturn caused by bad weather and allergies the group knows that if these five are at least spinning cord and weaving mats it will still substantially raise the wellbeing of all of them.

Regular Economy – A lot of time spent fishing and yam farming:

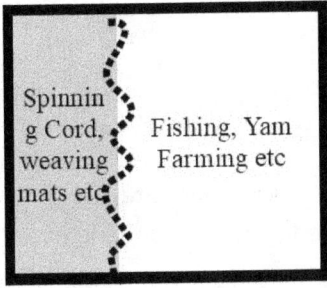

When there is bad weather or bad allergy conditions, the group gets other things done, spinning cord, weaving mats etc.:

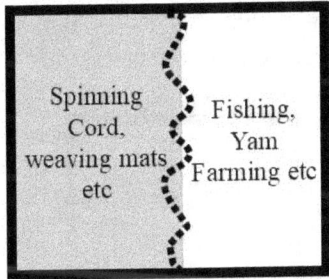

The fishers and allergy sufferers work at these much needed but slightly less urgent tasks until conditions improve, and then shift back into their normal work of fishing and yam farming when they can. At no point is it better for the group of ten castaways for the fishers and yam farmers to do nothing. It is a permanent loss to the castaway's wellbeing if these backup jobs are not done when they can be.

We can think of these projects as automatic backup projects. They are always beneficial to all, and whenever things slow down for any reason, there is no need for discussion or planning. Everyone that is temporarily freed up just starts in on these useful backup projects.

Some General Principles

WE HAVE SEEN HOW there are two systems for organizing economic activity. One increases private productivity, the other both creates goods that increase wellbeing that the private sector would not produce and amplifies the quantity of private production. How would a group such as our Islanders use these systems to reach the full capacity and maximum wellbeing for their society?

Think of the black box above again that represents the greatest possible productivity of the Island.

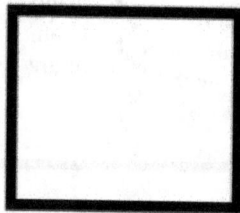

Each system is good at different things and serve different, non-overlapping tasks. We could try to fill the box with only public goods such as hospitals, parks, and infrastructure. But we would probably find that the resulting economy would be short of all the many things private businesses do well – providing abundant consumer goods, and a wide variety of choice, entertainment, restaurants, and other goods.

We could try to fill the box instead with only private

projects, but would probably find the resulting economy short on things we want such as national parks, a military, hospitals, pure research and education, and care for veterans and the elderly. Also, even the provision of abundant consumer goods would be less than it could be because public projects such as pure research, roads and infrastructure, education, and healthcare all greatly amplify the ability of private businesses to produce goods and services.

Additionally, however, it is unlikely that either system even could fill the box on its own, even if we were ideologically predisposed (as many people seem to be) against either a largely government or a largely private system. Because public projects amplify private activity, not doing them would leave this amplification process undone. In other words, the resulting economy would, by definition, be smaller than it could be.

So it seems best, just as we saw on our little ten person island, to have some mix of private and group projects in order to maximize wellbeing in society. But how do we know what mix?

One possibility might be to observe what projects are "naturally" public and do as many of these as able/desired. There are three basic reasons some goods are naturally public goods (adapted in part from Sekera 2014):

1. The market will not produce them because there is often not an effective market (examples: clean air, transport infrastructure, public sanitation, weather data collection, pure research, food and drug safety)

2. They are so beneficial to society as a whole that carrying them out is worth more than the resources needed to carry them out (public libraries, potable water, education, parks, fire and police protection, 911 call service)

3. A single provider is more efficient than multiple providers. This is often the case with networks, such as a national rail transport system, communications networks, and utilities (legal system, bank regulation, rail systems, networks in general).

Another possibility could be to "start" with System One. System One grows as banks fund activities that are successful. Assuming banks are good at their job (discussed further in Chapter 4: The Real World), System One will grow until there are no more productivity-raising projects to fund. We might say that the private system has a natural optimum size that is measurable to some degree based on the (healthy) amount of private debt/loans. When private banks grant all the loans to projects like John's fishing net that they believe can be successful, but no more, System One is at its optimal size. (Again, Chapter 4 considers the very real problems with the pronounced tendency for the finance sector to grow far larger than is healthy).

This is of course a simplistic statement of very basic principles, and the balance between public and private is a complex social outcome. In practice this will be one of the greatest debates the Islanders must have among themselves.

I MAGINE THAT INSTEAD OF the black box above representing all of the resources we desire to use from our economy, it is instead a large hot air balloon. A hot air balloon has a size limit it can expand to where it is at its most effective (by analogy, all desired resources are being used through good organization by Systems One and Two). When the hot air balloon is at its optimum it is full all the way but not bursting at the seams.

How would we fill this hot air balloon following the principles above?

We would begin to inflate it by encouraging the improvement of private activity, such as with John's fishing net in Chapter One. System One increases private activity to its maximum, as measured by all possible and desired productive loans being made but no more. A stable level of private debt that is being successfully repaid is the measure of the "right" size.

As we saw, this would most likely leave untapped resources and fail to coordinate many desirable social goods.

System Two would organize these group projects. Some of these directly inflate the balloon further (a hospital, for example, is new economic activity). Some inflate it indirectly by amplifying private production (a bridge increases the productivity of the producers in an area, a road in an area, healthcare of society in general, education in general in the long run, etc).

Public projects can be spent-in to the economy until the "balloon is fully inflated." This is measured by noting when prices begin to rise, meaning the limit of real resources has been reached. As if the hot air balloon were beginning to burst at its seams.

Historically, the worst cases of economic downturns in economies have been precisely when the economy is deflating - that is, there is not enough activity to maintain prices and overall economic activity.[5]

Keeping the economy fully inflated using whatever mix of System One and System Two a democracy decides on improves the wellbeing of everyone with no negative effects. We want the balloon to be perfectly full just like a hot air balloon for flying. We have all possible benefits of consumer goods from System One, and all possible benefits of public goods from System Two, but have not exceeded our desired real-resource use, so prices are stable.

A ND NOW, ONE LAST scenario: Imagine the hot air balloon is homemade, perhaps by some desperate single survivor on an island trying to get to civilization. It is pieced together like a quilt from any available materials sewn

_____

5 When prices are deflating from weak demand, people spend less, businesses earn less, people are laid off, so people spend less so businesses earn less... you get the idea. It creates a downward spiral that is much more dangerous and harmful to wellbeing than inflation. Debt-deflation, in turn, arises from the credit-money system. A corrupt system gives out loans that are unlikely to be productive, to the lender and borrowers short-term personal benefit. However, as this process causes the credit-money system to expand, it reaches a point where private debt can't be repaid anymore. As the economy slows down, the deflation scenario above happens, but is made much worse. Borrowers default on loans, which rapidly shrinks the balance sheets of lenders, meaning suddenly less credit-money in the system. This further exacerbates the problem, and more and more people default. This makes a debt-deflationary episode a very dramatic decline in the economy. Often a longer deflationary period is started first with debt-deflation then long-term deflation afterwards.

together, including old life-rafts and rain jackets a survivor has found. So its surface is not perfectly smooth.

So again we inflate the hot air balloon as far as we can with private industry, up to the point where no productive loans can be made. We inflate it the rest of the way with public projects that amplify private projects, provide social goods we want, and serve to keep the balloon inflated to its full potential. Deflation, as always, is the ever-present danger that can send the economy spiraling downward (making everyone far less well off).

However, the last little uneven bits—the bits shaped like the life raft or sleeves of the raincoat, are still a little saggy. To get them to fill all the way out to the very maximum lifting-potential of our balloon, we could try to keep inflating the balloon with still more public projects. But to get the amount of pressure needed to fill those bits out would cause too much pressure on the overall balloon and it would begin to split at the seams. In other words, in trying to fill the economy with a last bit of activity we would begin to exceed the amount of available real resources and begin to experience inflation before we would manage to have everyone who wants to work to have a task.

We could just leave those last bits of the balloon unfilled rather than risk over-inflating our balloon.

However, in our analogy, the last bits represent unemployment, like the deep sea fishers during storms or the asthma sufferers in the example above. Filling them in gives us some last available increases in public goods (spinning cord in the example above). As crusoes are never scarce, not using these last resources is always a waste.

But more importantly, these last resources are humans,

not materials. Unemployment is a unique problem, different than merely leaving some desired public projects undone. Leaving some machines or raw materials idle means less than full capacity, but only that specific loss.

Leaving people idle contributes directly to some of the worst and most costly problems any society faces. "Inflating our balloon" to get that last little bit filled is therefore doubly useful. We gain some otherwise un-done public goods like clean parks, companionship for the elderly, staffing far more numerous animal shelters etc. And we directly target the huge social problem that is unemployment.

The analogy would be somehow directly injecting gas into those last little pockets of our balloon, thereby inflating the last little bits that regular pressure can't get to.

In addition to (1) not throwing away a free opportunity to achieve desirable social goals like clean parks and elderly care, there are four other reasons the Islanders have automatic backup projects for the unemployed:

2. The second reason is that unemployment has been shown by sociologists, doctors and psychologists to have extremely high social costs. The unemployed lose skills permanently, and are far more prone to addictive and abusive behavior. Most people take pride in a job well done, and when willing workers are denied this opportunity, communities and families suffer. The real costs of unemployment-related addictions, abuse, and skill loss is staggering. These are also permanent losses to society and permanent losses to future generations as children grow up in abusive households or households with addiction, lower education, and related problems.

3. One possible problem with attempting to maximize material wellbeing by just trying to increase public projects is that this could be slow and unresponsive. The Islanders would need to meet, decide on projects, and might get bogged down arguing about details. However, automatic backups kick-in instantly with no debate. Just like spinning cord – there are a lot of park maintenance, basic infrastructure, tutoring, elderly care/companionship (reading, visiting, helping with daily tasks) and many other jobs that are always useful, needed, and generally involve some tasks that do not require extensive training. Newly unemployed can automatically go into these positions with no new debates by the group. Thus useful things get done straight away, the unemployed person is not unemployed for long, and crusoes are directed immediately to the cohort or region of the Island where they are needed. This brings us to...

4. A fourth reason is that in larger societies, unlike a small island of ten castaways, unemployment is spread spatially unevenly across a country and among its population. Simply trying to increase private production or even public production is not targeted; raising overall production will likely still leave some cohorts or regions with unemployed. Having automatic backup projects always ready means that they "kick in" exactly where they are needed and for whom they are needed. If a mining region, for example, becomes unprofitable and begins to suffer high unemployment, directly employing those newly unemployed in that region means helping that region and that type of worker directly.

This is not easy to do by simply increasing general spending on public projects.

5. Fifth, this automatic stabilizing effect for cohorts and regions works for the whole economy, stabilizing it. Complex economies like our Island (and especially our real world) can be prone to swings in price levels. This is made much worse if, in a downturn, people go from some (even low) wage to a zero wage (complete unemployment). This can set off a cycle where the unemployed can't spend, businesses sell less, they lay off more workers, and so on. And upswings can be too exuberant (potentially causing price rises) if suddenly the unemployed go from zero to full wages and start spending.

It is much better for stability if in a downturn, the newly unemployed still make a living wage. They keep spending, businesses keep selling, and the downturn is mild. If things get better, they go from the backup project rate to a private sector wage, a much smaller jump, so there is little inflationary swing. Having automatic backup work serves to greatly reduce swings that can occur as people fall into unemployment.

We are better off in every way if we directly employ the unemployed. Just as all would spin cord and weave mats on the ten person island, we should enable everyone who wants to to be able to work on all the endless tasks we are behind on in our real economies as well. As long as there are real resources available, there are always crusoes (ledger entries) to organize work on these tasks. No one should be forced to be idle because of an erroneous belief that there is not enough "money." (Much of the above discussion on automatic stabilizers derives from the general academic writing of economist Bill Mitchell at The University of Newcastle, Australia; see also the general work of economists L. Randall Wray at The University of Missouri-Kansas City and Pavlina R. Tcherneva at Bard College).

So there are five key reasons to have automatic backup projects: 1) Not having them is a permanent loss to society for no reason. 2) Not having them allows social ills from unemployment. This is a permanent and needless damage to future generations as well 3) Back up projects are fast and do not involve normal slow complex group decision making 4) Back up projects automatically help regions and cohorts. 5) Backup projects increase the stability of the economy not only for free, but with the benefits of 1-4. Not having them is a permanent loss - both now and to future generations - of wellbeing to society.

PART II

THE REAL WORLD

CHAPTER 4

THE REAL WORLD:
SYSTEM ONE
(HORIZONTAL)

We have seen how our Island of 1000 Castaways
developed an economy that, within the potential of their technology and resources, maximizes their wellbeing.

Our real-world economies are not organized so efficiently,
and create countries where wellbeing is, given some set of
resources and technology, less than it could be.

Why?

There are two primary reasons:

1. The Islanders efficiently manage System One, allowing it to grow to its maximum useful size but no more.
In the real world we allow the finance sector to be much
larger than is efficient, with everything beyond its maximum size reducing rather than raising wellbeing.

2. The Islanders understand how to use System Two. In
the real world, quite simply, we do not.

System One

THE PRIMARY REASON FOR "1" above is simply that the
wealthy are able to change the rules of banking and
finance in their own favor. This creates a snowball effect
where they become still wealthier with more political influence, change the rules a little bit more and so on, until the
system becomes so out of touch with the real economy that it
collapses. This effect is portrayed on the first page of this
Chapter, where the monopolists and cartels of the late 1800s
are pulling the strings of U.S. lawmaking. However, as powerful as those interests were at that time, the feedback mech-
anism today is even more direct and accordingly still
stronger, with finance and banking powers changing the
rules of the very finance system itself. Finance is a flow managing our real resources; the wealthy are able to tap directly
into that stream and siphon off ever more unearned ledger
entries that can then be exchanged for unearned real wealth,

at everyone else's expense, not least, the integrity of the public governmental system.[6]

This process is aided by a natural tendency for private finance towards instability. As the economy becomes stronger due to efficient production generated from System One, it seems that loans do not default easily, so more projects are funded with less and less scrupulous attention to their real worth, until the system becomes dominated by poor loans and a high degree of private debt. The health of the overall system gets bad enough that finally some people default, the economies gets worse, and a cascade of default

---

6 A basic issue of democracy is that of special interests. This was a concern of the founders of the United States in The Federalist Papers (Federalist No. 10 by James Madison) and a central political-economic theory of the fall of nations (Mancur Olson's *The Rise and Decline of Nations*). The concern is that governments are designed in part to protect the rights of the individual. But individuals band together to create groups within a larger society. It is easy for some groups to become more powerful than others, to the extent that the original purpose of democracy is undermined (where powerful groups in effect control society and the very idea of democracy no longer functions as intended).

Some special interests are unique, in that their particular interest is the very political and economic system itself. Unlike, say, outdoor enthusiasts who advocate for more parks, this special kind of special interest is focused on the very laws concerning power and finance. If these power- and finance-focused special interests succeed in their goal of changing rules to benefit themselves, this process can easily exhibit positive feedback. They influence the system in a way that makes them more able to influence it again and so on. This is manifested in the macroeconomy by creating a system that favors the wealthy and politically powerful in what becomes a runaway process. To summarize:

-Playing the game is fine.

-Changing the rules of the game in your favor is not fine.

-Changing the rules in your favor, then using your newfound influence and wealth to change the rules over and over ever more in your favor = a recipe for disaster.

and debt-deflation occurs.

On the upside of this cycle, the tendency for the wealthy to influence the rules of financing and banking reinforce the natural tendency for finance to grow too large. This occurs as the wealthy benefit from the growth (as bankers, real estate speculators, investors, lawyers for these, and so on), while at the same time the growth grants them unearned wealth by which to influence the rules ever more.

How does the Island avoid the problem of the finance sector growing unhealthily large, burdening the economy by poor investments, private defaults, and through channeling vast sums of unearned wealth to a small finance-related minority? It does so by sticking to "plain vanilla" banking and finance, to the basics of banking that work and no more.

Banking and finance are ancient and what works—and what does not—despite the protestations of those who gain from obfuscation, is well understood. Anyone claiming that banking and finance are "too complex" to regulate or that "financial innovation is vital" is someone who stands to gain unearned wealth (at everyone else's expense) from the increased complexity.

Rule number one, then, is to keep banking and finance simple and thus transparent. Rather than allowing the finance sector to "innovate," and then later trying to manage the fallout by scrambling around creating new regulations, the Island's government instead tells banks from the outset what they are allowed to do, and then makes them ask to do anything different. Quite simply, banks are public charters created to fund productive enterprises and run our payments system, and should do nothing else.

There are several other common sense ways that, although seemingly simple, actually make the Island banking system profoundly more sound than our real-world banking systems. These include, in addition to "1" above (this list is largely adapted from Warren Mosler 2009, suggested after the crisis of 2008):

2. Banks must keep the loans they make on their own books until cleared. This simple rule makes sure banks carefully consider the quality of each project they lend to. It also makes sure banks will operate locally with local knowledge, as there is no easy way judge the quality of many loans without knowing a location and industry well.

3. Banks are be allowed to lend only directly to borrowers, and only for capital development purposes (i.e. business credit lines and household loans).

4. Banks are not be allowed to engage in profit making ventures beyond basic lending; banks should profit through high quality credit analysis, nothing else (they serve no other useful purpose, besides the payment system). The public allows banks to operate because they can increase overall wellbeing in the way John's fishing nets did. There is no reason to allow them to profit from their special powers for any other reason.

5. Banks must operate on a single balance sheet, and with no subsidiaries of any kind. This serves to make them vastly more transparent.

6. Banks cannot accept financial assets as collateral.

Stopping financial leverage reduces the potential for instability and debt-deflation, as well as reduces the transfer of unearned wealth to the wealthy from a bloated finance system not based on the real economy. Financial leverage does not contribute to the purpose of banks, which is to aid in the organization of capital-increasing projects in the private sector.

7. Banks should not be allowed to buy (or sell) credit default insurance. Default insurance takes away the proper incentives to earn only from high quality credit analysis. The lender should lose (due to making an unwise loan).

These basic rules, although very simple, vastly shrink the banking/finance sector (as only high quality loans are made) and make it far more healthy and stable. This in turn significantly raises wellbeing via another avenue: A smaller finance sector means much less private debt, which translates into greater real wellbeing for the average citizen.

[Note - a primary means by which unearned wealth is transferred to the already wealthy is via a poorly regulated finance sector. However, another key avenue is via allowing monopolies or oligopolies to form; these are able to charge higher prices (profit) than they otherwise would be able with proper regulation and a healthy system of smaller companies. Both finance and large companies need regulation to minimize unearned real-resource transfer to the wealthy. Note that breaking up natural monopolies in businesses that are inherently about networks (communications, transport) is generally not possible; the only way to serve society in those industries is through government ownership or regulation]

Our real-world economies provide much less wellbeing than they could simply because the above rules are either not in existence or are not enforced. This allows the banking and finance sector to grow far larger than needed to carry out its purpose. This leads to financial instability and debt-deflation. It leads to the psychological and practical hardships of too much private debt for citizens. It leads to a corrupted political system. It causes the banking sector to grow so large that it funnels money into assets, inflating their value, which in turn further rewards unearned wealth to the wealthy and prices housing (especially) out of reach of normal citizens. (The banking sector nets to zero, but its total size matters as well).

The drag on the economy from a poorly run, bloated, parasitic System One is the single greatest burden on real-world economies, reducing wellbeing below potential.

Except for one.
We turn to it now.

CHAPTER 5

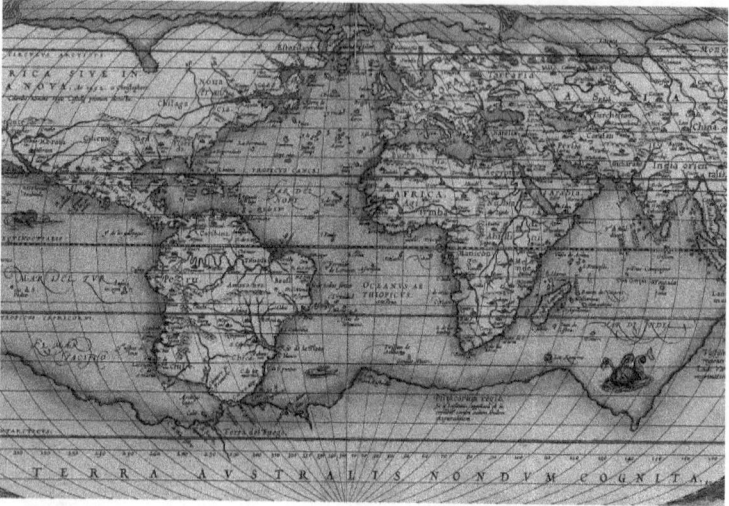

THE REAL WORLD: SYSTEM TWO (VERTICAL)

T he other main reason our real-world economies do not function as well as the Island is that we simply do not understand System Two, which organizes public projects and creates the vertical component of modern currency systems. The reasons for this stem from the long, complex process by which our modern economies emerged.

It might be expected that I will say that the inherited *structure* of our real-world System Two is sub-optimal and must be changed for our economy to run as efficiently as the Island economy. *But the primary problem is actually our inherited beliefs*, not structure.

The Island developed in isolation and quickly developed the most advanced version of System Two possible. Its imaginary small population is well-informed on how it developed and how it functions. And thus, most crucially, the 1000 Castaways are able to elect representatives who likewise understand how to use System Two correctly, and do so.

As we know, public projects are the democratic transfer of private resources to desired public projects. On the Island the public and the representatives they choose to guide their System Two know that the "cost" of these projects (and the ability to carry them out) is measured in real resources. The "funding" of these projects occurs the moment they vote to do the project, that is, the moment they make the decision to put their real resources towards something. They "fund" a road when they decide together to build it, not with abstract numbers in a ledger that they themselves create. The ledger-entries are merely an organizing tool.

The small ten person island from the Introduction makes this clear. If ten people decide to build a dining hut together, the cost is the labor and materials on their island, and the "funding" is when they decide to do it. They do not need any organizing tool because their "society" is so small. The greater size of the 1000 Castaways Island and our modern real societies means the organizing tool is needed, but does not change the fact that real resources are the only cost and the decision to carry out a project is the funding.

The Islanders know that of course they will "spend-in" (create) more ledger entries of crusoes than they will tax out, for the simple reason that people will want to save some tax-credits (crusoes) to feel secure, to invest or carry out their own projects, and to postpone consumption.

This saving process of crusoes is a good for the Islanders, improving their wellbeing (their sense of security, expectation of future agency, etc.). Spending-in (creating new) ledger entries of crusoes always equals the taxing out of crusoes plus the savings of crusoes, with the health of the vertical system judged only by its ability to organize public projects.

On the Island, note the following beliefs and practices:

1. The Islanders can directly save and transact in their own tax-credits.

2. The Islanders know that, like a lump of gold in a safe, saved tax-credits do not earn interest (it is *vacua pecunia*). If Islanders want to earn a return on their saved money they invest their savings in System One projects like John's fishing nets.

3. The Islanders know the primary tools for managing their economy are a) making sure System One is healthy (which amounts to the same thing as it being the optimal size, i.e., with minimal private debt) and b) keeping the economy fully inflated and fully employed by carrying out all desired public projects that real resources allow.

4. As mentioned, the Islanders understand that the amount saved by them is not harmful (it is good for them to have the security of savings) as long as the value of ledger entries and equality of savings (no hoarding by a faction of ultra-rich) is the right amount to maintain the integrity of both their financial and their governmental system.

In our real-world economies we have inherited a different set of beliefs and practices on all of these points. The public and its elected representatives in our world believe or practice (note that below, "1" in part causes or encourages "4", and that "2" causes or encourages "3"):

1. Modern citizens cannot directly save and transact in their own tax-credits. Thus, in order to save them directly, they must convert their tax-credits into a different type of government ledger-entry called "securities" or "bonds."

2. It is generally thought that savers should be paid to save this different type of government ledger entry (i.e., that the government should pay them interest). Note that paying interest on bonds means the government raises the base rate of lending/borrowing in the economy. The government can raise or lower this rate at will by paying more or less interest on government bonds.

3. Most elected officials are taught and thus act as if the above manipulation of the base interest rate is the

primary tool for managing the economy. They focus on tiny manipulations of this rate[7] rather than focus on questions of how to best use System Two. This contrasts with the Island where System Two is the primary point of discussion of how to maximize the economy of the Island. Preoccupation with government manipulation of interest rates does not happen at all on the Island since the Island government does not pay interest on saved tax-credits.

4. That savings in this alternative government ledger-entry ("bonds") are somehow a problem ("debt").

---

7 The belief that manipulating the base interest rate is useful stems primarily from the effect that lowering rates increases private borrowing (inflating the economy some) and raising rates decreases private borrowing (cooling the economy some). However, a healthy System One should be above all stable, with private debt remaining minimal and beneficial. Among other problems, decreasing the interest rate encourages borrowing in the short term, yet guarantees lower injections of money in the future (less interest payments), opposing forces on demand. Interest rate increases raise the cost of borrowing in the short term, but inject money into the economy later - again, opposing forces on demand. Also, interest rate increases, which are meant to cool the economy and reduce price rises, get added into pricing by business, raising prices. The impact over the short- and medium-term are opposite and work against each other, making interest rate adjustments fail to achieve their purpose, while causing other harmful effects to the economy. Also, interest rate changes are not generally that important in the decision of buyers, except the housing market. This increases something we don't want - housing becoming an asset for the wealthy to invest in rather than actually housing for normal people. The manipulation and its effects working against each other also causes unnecessary complexity in analyzing the economy (always harmful). Automatic stabilizers are more fair, fast and reliable in every way.

The inherited real-world beliefs and practices 1-4 are the opposite of the Island's beliefs and practices. The last of these, "4", that the public believes that governments have a debt (or must avoid going into debt), is the single greatest hindrance to running the economy efficiently. "3" above abets this hindrance by misleading the public into believing something useful is being done when in fact it is not.

This straitjackets the economy into a guaranteed sub-optimal performance, as we miss out on public projects, we miss out on the amplification effect on private production from public projects, and we miss out on the five automatic-stabilizer benefits of full employment (like spinning cord on the ten person Island).

The main point of this book, then, is simply to show why "4" above occurs and why it is false. There is no constraint from our ledger system, no "monetary" or "debt" constraint, on carrying out public projects. Absolutely none. *Running System Two with a belief other than the understanding that we use infinite ledger entries only as an organizing tool is the single most dangerous mistaken belief that we have inherited.*

It does not actually matter how this misconception came about, just that it did. It is evident in our textbooks, our newscasts and newspaper headlines, in discussions by normal concerned citizens, by the teachers in our classrooms, from high school to the most prestigious graduate programs in economics.

And it is simply wrong.

A false belief that our ledger system constrains us, combined with the political problem outlined in the previous chapter (Chapter 4) are, by far, the primary reasons developed economies perform worse than they could. If Chapters 1 through 5 are understood, the solutions are clear. We can change our beliefs and take the last evolutionary steps to economies that run as well as is possible. The only constraints on our wellbeing then become technological.

Addendum: The Emerged Economy

SEALING OF THE BANK OF ENGLAND CHARTER. 1694.
Sir John Houblon.   Sir John Somers.   Mr. Michael Godfrey
Governor.   Lord Keeper.   Deputy Governor.

T HE BASIC POINT OF this book concludes above. However, understanding how we have gotten to where we are is nonetheless fascinating in and of itself. Moreover, it just might help shed some light on how to take the final steps towards ridding ourselves of misconceptions on the economy, and thus electing representatives who are capable of organizing our economies rationally.

So, how did real-world economies come to have these dysfunctional beliefs?

Remember, first, that there are two basic possibilities for how our modern mix of a private and public system (System

One and System Two, creating horizontal and vertical money respectively), sharing the same unit of account, could arise:

1. A government demands some penalty, fine, tax, or tribute, giving value to a unit of account that can then also become the unit of account for a private system of banking.

2. A pre-existing private currency (of any kind) is co-opted by an emerging state. All the state (with its monopoly on force in its territory) has to do is begin demanding taxes in the pre-existing unit; to the extent it is effective at taxation, then the old unit becomes the new tax-credit of the new state, taking on a life of its own within that territory (soon becoming distinguished from its older precursor, to control it completely within that state, creating a completely new unit of account, often with the same name as an older currency or measure (This process of the rise of independent tax-systems causing splits from older units of account is evident in the many distinct currencies sharing versions of older names, i.e., the many versions and related unit-of-account "families." E.g., guilder/florin, franc, marks, denarius/libra/livre/lira/pound, riksdaler, crown/krona, yen/won/yuan).

The new state now has a System One and a System Two, both sharing the old unit of account, which is now a tax-credit unique to the new country (polity/state).

From either of these emerge a system like that of the Island, with a System One and System Two sharing the same unit of account, a tax-credit.

Emergence

OUR MODERN STATES AND state-system largely date from the second millennium (11th to 20th centuries), especially taking off from about ~1500 AD. States at this time began developing much more effective bureaucracies and tax systems. In the same time period and region (western Eurasia) banking, insurance, credit, and trade systems were also developing into their modern forms, with early forms of bills of exchange and similar ledger entries of credit and double-entry bookkeeping.

These innovative new polities out-competed their rivals and became our modern states/countries. In their early stages a number of them used the new financial innovations. Indeed, these financial methods may have been the very thing that allowed them to out-compete older political forms.

How did this work?

Basically, just like a growing new business, these growing early proto-states borrowed some already established currency to help them grow. During the same time period they were also becoming effective at taxation. Crucially, once they were able to tax effectively, they could in theory do (2) above, co-opting whatever unit was common in their territory, thus creating a System Two alongside and linked with an existing System One, and then running their economy exactly as the Island does, spending (creating) tax-credits directly. However, this was not widely recognized over the ensuing centuries. Indeed, we are still in the very midst of this process coming to its final stage: the understanding that we can run a

System Two exactly like the Island. As we have noted—the change in finance and currency institutions and practices occur at a glacial pace (and the understanding of these lags behind still more).

How does it work?

First, a proto-state without its own currency: There is some regionally accepted earlier currency that it wants more of to pay a military or mercenaries, and for other vital public projects (this is just like the process of John's fishing nets, except writ large to polities).

The proto-state writes up ledger entries of promises-to-pay to its lenders. They accept these newly written ledger entries, and the proto-state receives the already-existing currency. If the proto-state is successful, it is able to pay back the lenders and retire the promissory notes.

Once it is successful and has a monopoly on force in its territory and an effective bureaucracy that can tax effectively, it becomes able to run like the Island. But because of its inherited beliefs, it still issues "bonds."

How does this work?

The new country wants to carry out new public (System Two) projects beyond what currency it has on its books. So like before, it creates out-of-thin-air promissory notes ("bonds") that it will "sell" (swap) for already existing currency (tax-credits) already held by savers. (They do not fund anything, and in fact serve as annuities,[8] with their only possible useful role related to pensions, discussed below). These savers eagerly accept this deal because the new "bonds" (annuities) pay interest. They swap their already existing saved currency for the bonds/annuities. The new country marks up its public account by this same number, and then spends in that amount of tax-credits into the economy to pay for public projects. These are of course accepted as the public always desires to earn tax-credits as they are the only form of demonstrating their contribution to System Two (just like the Island).

This is exactly the system that modern states use. They create bonds out of thin air. These are eagerly accepted by savers of tax-credits, since the bonds pay interest. That number is marked up to the government's ledger, and this number of tax-credits is then spent back in to the economy on public projects.

Note, however, that this project is, accounting-wise, exactly as if the government just directly spent tax-credits into the economy to carry out public projects like the Island does, and then paid savers of tax-credits an annuity.

In other words, it is exactly like the Island system accounting-wise, even in the real world, except paying annu-

---

8 Annuity: from French *annuité*, Latin *annuus*: "yearly." A sum of money paid to someone each year, often for insurance and pension purposes. A sovereign government never needs to sell bonds for funds; it might, however, decide to sell some annuities to provide safe retirement savings. An annuity may mimic other payments like dividends, profit, or interest, but this does not make it a stock or bond (although after a Roman period as a pension type instrument, the word was used in medieval times in a way similar to the modern idea of a bond (as were tontines and forms of lotteries), and then reverted largely back to being associated with pensions in modern usage).

ities to savers.

The Island does not need this annuity payment because it takes care of pensions and healthcare directly (transparent and efficient). And savers are allowed to keep and access their tax-credits on the public ledger, and thus can save 100% safely without the need to change their tax-credits to some other instrument. It also does not need to manipulate interest rates to manipulate System One, since System One is maintained at a steady healthy size as outlined in Chapter 4.

We can run our economies like the Island with no structural changes simply by realizing that "bonds" are merely savings, and that tweaking the base interest rate is not useful. This would still leave the annuity/bonds and an artificially elevated base interest rate, but the most important part - maintaining an adequate amount of System Two projects to fully inflate the economy - could be carried out even with the inherited baggage of an illusory "bond" system.

The best modern economists argue for this possibility. That is, even though we have to deal with the existing but archaic (and accounting-wise, meaningless) bond system, we can do a "work around" and actually just run the system in the way the Island does.

A problem, however, with maintaining our existing complex structure and just running it like the Island is that it may be too complicated for the public to ever grasp. Better to simply let our system evolve to its final rational form, the form the Island has. This would mean creating good enough pensions, welfare, and health care that savers and institutions would not be dependent on government annuities. What needs that do remain can then be managed with targeted annuities created directly for pensions and related purposes, a much smaller system whose purpose is transparent, unlike the current byzantine system. We could in effect lower the interest rate on bonds to zero. But this in turn makes evident the very pointlessness of our vestigial "bond" system: With zero interest there is no good reason a saver would trade saved tax-credits to "bonds" in the first place.

So the obvious thing to do is spend tax-credits directly (always valued because they are tax-credits) and do away with bonds.

Besides their pension function and the myth that interest-rate propping-up/easing-of-propping-up is somehow useful, there is the inherited belief that forcing savers to convert their savings to bonds stops a large "money supply" from being inflationary. However, those who buy bonds planned to save already, so changing them to bonds does nothing. This is doubly so as bonds are highly liquid and can "act" as money almost as easily as savings accounts can.

Directly spending tax-credits rather than creating "bonds" first is not inflationary. Precisely because they are tax-credits. Sadly, this is generally not grasped by modern economists who haven't yet understood the manner in which sovereign tax-credits made sovereign bonds obsolete several centuries ago.

Accounting-wise we virtually already run on a system like the Island system. The main problems we have running our System Two properly are inherited beliefs. However, the transparency of the entire system is deeply hindered by the details of the inherited structure. For this reason alone, given that it is the public who must run the economy via their representatives, it is imperative to have the clearest system possible.

THE SLINGS AND ARROWS OF OUTRAGEOUS FORTUNE
(Additional Material, Chapter Five)

Consider our little Island with its well-balanced System One and System Two. What if instead it had had to grow its little economy in the midst of 9 other islands?

If they were 9 other completely peaceful Islands, and all endowed with the same abundant materials and climate that our Island had, things might have worked out about the same, for all 10 islands.

But imagine the other 9 islands had constant, murderous intent to invade your little island. Now there would be a sustained need to raise and maintain a military. Now imagine that often they were your immediate land neighbors rather than distant islands, generally ready to march into your territory, and often larger, richer, and more powerful than you.

Now further imagine that there are large differences in

the amounts and types of raw materials between different territories. And your territory might have lacked not some but perhaps even most of the basics needed to feed and house and clothe a growing population. From the earliest stages of emerging states there would exist strong pressures for "international" trade and with that many added layers of complexity such as many different types of "money" (from commodity-based coins to various types of notes of credit) and thus foreign exchange, bills of exchange, and other complex credit- and insurance- instruments related to long-distance trade. [note that "commodity based coins" themselves were rarely if ever {ingot form} actually valued for their commodity value - the value was in practice from taxation/fine/tribute or the use of precious metals was a form of anti- counterfeiting, making "fakes" difficult, but not giving the actual value to the coins]

The proto-states that are the precursors to modern states developed in a world that was much more like this latter scenario than our peaceful, abundant little Island.

Imagine again that you are part of a small region or city-state with an emerging state structure in this environment. Long-distance and large-scale trade already exist, and with them, large and often powerful merchant banks and merchant companies are developing such as the Dutch East India Company and the English East India Company. You are also surrounded by despots, large and power-

ful Merchant Companies (quasi-states in their own way), the Hanseatic League, kingdoms large and small, fading empires, rising empires, weak, flailing states, tribute states, mercenaries, huge, ancient religious institutions.

Many of these polities, institutions, companies and banks are larger, older, and better organized than your own proto-state is. What we in hindsight know became modern nation states often initially had a minimally organized bureaucracy and were barely able to impose a tax on its people or provide services. And they were at constant threat of invasion or incorporation into other political units.

Out of this swirling melee emerged the modern state, a form whose initial stirrings are in the mid second millennium in far western Eurasia and really taking off after 1800. Eventually, proto-states became our modern sovereign states – often relatively large, well-organized bureaucratically, able to sustain a military, sustain taxation, and carry out international trade (and often, grew to a size and complexity where it could provide itself with a great deal of its needs). Once these developed, they were able to tax and circulate tax-credits as money.

After the dawn of agriculture it took something like 7,000 years for the Classical polities of the Middle East, China, and the early Greeks and then Romans to begin to have some of the characteristics that modern states developed (around perhaps 1000 BC) – semi-efficient tax systems and early forms of banking. There was then a decline or at least a lull in much of the world in these activities in the early first Millennium. It then took another millennia or more for the stirrings of the modern nation-state that would lead to the full tax-credit and banking systems of modern nation states around the world today.

In other words, it took something like 9,000 years from the beginnings of agriculture to the emergence of modern nation states after about 1800 AD with increasingly modern banking and taxation systems. What seems now like obvious ways to organize a society was not at all easy in actual fact.

Similarly, despite modern nation states achieving the ability to run Vertical and Horizontal systems like the Island at about that time (they could circulate tax credits and modern banking was practiced), it took what is relatively a small amount of time but still several centuries for these systems to be understood, a process which we are in the middle of still in 2019.

Dates for these developments are purposefully general since there are differing definitions of the institution and variance around the world.

We can grasp the intense competition early groups in the real world faced (unlike our isolated 1000 Castaways) with the following maps. The first is from 301 BC, the numerous social groups (linguistic, ethnic, tribal, proto-nations etc.)

Western Eurasia in 300 BC, 1092 AD, and 1648 AD:

Western Eurasian Tribes, c. 300 BC

Western Eurasian Polities, 1092 AD

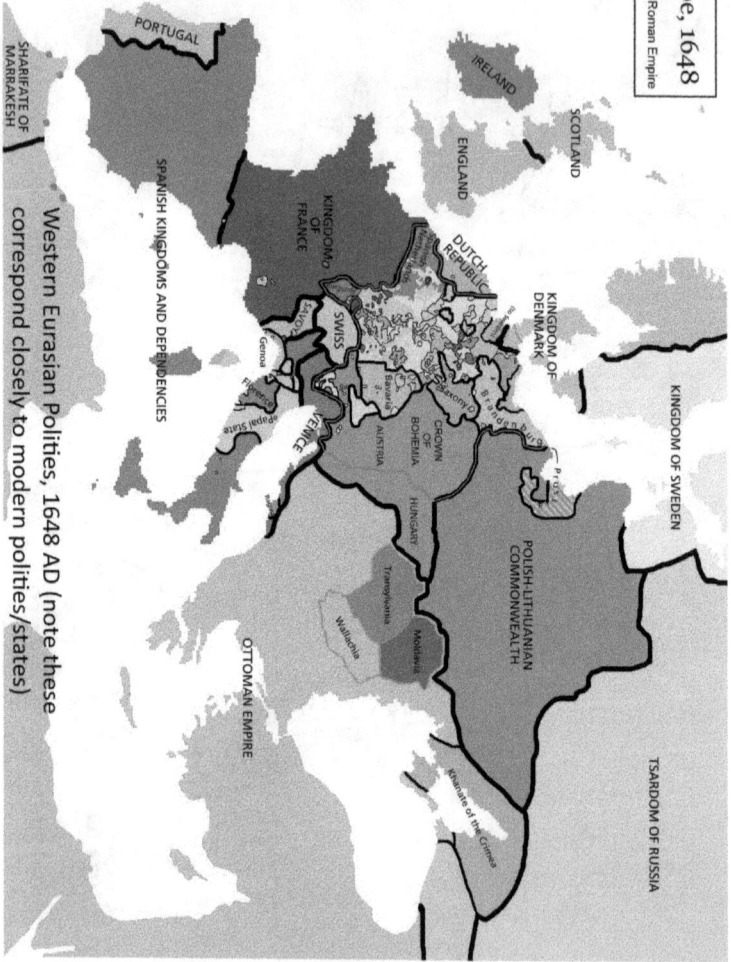

Europe, 1648
—— Holy Roman Empire

Western Eurasian Polities, 1648 AD (note these correspond closely to modern polities/states)

PORTUGAL
IRELAND
SCOTLAND
ENGLAND
SHARIFATE OF MARRAKESH
SPANISH KINGDOMS AND DEPENDENCIES
KINGDOM OF FRANCE
DUTCH REPUBLIC
KINGDOM OF DENMARK
KINGDOM OF SWEDEN
SWISS
Savoy
Genoa
Florence
Papal States
VENICE
Bavaria
Saxony
Brandenburg
Prussia
AUSTRIA
CROWN OF BOHEMIA
HUNGARY
POLISH-LITHUANIAN COMMONWEALTH
TSARDOM OF RUSSIA
Transylvania
Wallachia
Moldavia
Khanate of the Crimea
OTTOMAN EMPIRE

It is clear that our real world has gone through a much longer and far more violent, complex institutional development than the 1000 Castaways endured. Our "modern" economics reflect this: *only a handful of economists have grasped the full ramifications of running our system on tax-credits and the utter obsoleteness of "sovereign bonds."*

WORKS CITED

Graeber, David. *Debt: The First 5,000 Years*. Melville House, New York.

(See also the fascinating, somewhat related work by Michael Hudson (2018) *..and forgive them their debts: Lending, Foreclosure and Redemption From Bronze Age Finance to the Jubilee Year.* ISLET, Dresden.)

Mosler, Warren and Mathew Forstater. 1999. "A General Analytical Framework for the Analysis of Currencies and Other Commodities." in *Full Employment and Price Stability in a Global Economy*, Paul Davidson and Jan Kregel, eds. Edward Elgar, Cheltenham, UK.

Mosler, Warren. 2009. "Proposals for the Banking System, Treasury, Fed, and FDIC (draft)".

http://moslereconomics-kg5winhhtut.stackpathdns.com/wp-content/pdfs/Proposals.pdf.

Olson, Mancur 1982. *The Rise and Decline of Nations: Economic Growth, Stagflation, and Social Rigidities*. New Haven: Yale University Press. 1982.

Sekera, June. 2014. Re-thinking the Definition of "Public Goods" Real-World Economics Review Blog. July 9th, 2014.

Strauss, Ilana E. 2016. "The Myth of the Barter Economy: Adam Smith said that quid-pro-quo exchange systems preceded economies based on currency, but there's no evidence that he was right." *The Atlantic*.

THE END

A FEW POINTS ON "QUANTITATIVE EASING," MMT, TRADE POLICY, & ECONOMIC GEOGRAPHY

"Quantitative Easing"

After the debt-deflation of 2008, mainstream economists were scrambling around trying to do something useful, although their empty economics made this impossible. One thing they tried is what they called "quantitative easing." They believed that by having the government buy bond holdings of banks (replacing the banks' bonds with reserves [vertical money], and thus increasing their government "vertical" tax-credit holdings) they could stimulate the economy.

Why? They believed that if the banks had more vertical money they would lend more, which would in turn stimulate the economy. This is the false "loanable funds" idea I said we would come back to in Chapter 1.

However, as we know, banks do not sit around and wait for reserves in order to then lend them on. They create "promises to pay" out of thin air for any customers who are creditworthy.

The problem after a debt-deflation like 2008 is that there has been a growth of far too much private credit-money. There are very few people able or willing to borrow more.

Thus, having the banks have more reserves—despite the massive amounts added—did essentially nothing to stimulate the economy. All it does in effect is switch bank holdings from a savings account at the Federal Reserve, to a checking account at the Federal Reserve.

The public had few people left who wanted loans who had not already taken them out, and indeed, with much worse economic conditions, there was both much less reason to take out loans for new projects, and the people's financial shape was much worse off, making them worse credit risks.

A Note On MMT And International Trade

Our focus in economics, as we have discussed throughout this book, should always be on real resources (or how finance affects these, something mainstream economics neglects, making it essentially useless).

To this point important Modern Monetary Theorists have sometimes made a counter-intuitive and arresting point: exporting is a real loss to a country, and importing is a real gain (with the caveat that we are at full employment, something that often gets forgotten). In other words, forgetting about "finance," if you are sending real goods away from your country you are "losing" something; if ships loaded with real resources are arriving on your shores then you are gaining something. The traditional view that "selling stuff" is good for the country (because it improves the overall "balance of trade" position of a country) and importing too much is bad has it all backward.

Some people automatically balk at this interesting view for overly simple reasons. However, within the framework of "normal" economics it is an astute, interesting point.

However, there is an important body of heterodox economics on trade, apart from MMT, sometimes known as The

Other Canon, perhaps best represented by the work of Erik Reinert. It shows how, when judging trade, it is crucial not just to look at dollar amounts, but at types of industries. Basically, there is a crucial difference between high-technology and raw materials/low-technology industries.

The MMT view would be astute in a neoclassical setting – which assumes that a sale is a sale and a product worth X dollars is the same as a different product worth X dollars. Neoclassical economics sees factor price equalization under a system of free trade making everyone better off, like Adam Smith's pin factory.

However, the world is marked by high agglomeration of high-tech industries, due to falling transport costs combining with knowledge-spillovers (local positive externalities). There is extreme disequilibrium. It is simply not the same to export raw materials or low-tech items as it is to export high-tech items (and thus concentrating high-tech industry in your territory). And worse still of course to need to import both.

Quite simply, exporting high-tech goods means concentrating high-tech industry within your territory. Not doing so means losing it. The consequences of this are profound.

The very top of the currency food chain is the US dollar. It can be "exported" like a raw-material (Indeed, dollars or other tax-credits trade like a commodity; see Mosler and Forstater 1999, "once a token is declared necessary for the payment of taxes it can be analyzed like any other commodity", p. 166). The cost, however, is losing high-tech industries. It is, in the long-term, a bad strategy. In the long-run it is best to not just maintain some semblance of parity between the value of exports and imports, but much more importantly, to maintain high-tech manufacturing. This leads to good jobs and a strong economy (and potential military might if needed). Not doing so guarantees a slow decline in the variety and quality of jobs, productivity, income, and military potential.

Importing low-tech while exporting high-tech is good for an economy. You get a lot of raw materials or cheap goods for a small amount of exported high-tech. And much more importantly, you tip the disequilibrium of agglomeration in your favor, attracting more high-paying, desirable, varied jobs (that also increase military potential if that is a worry). If you do the opposite, that is, export largely raw materials (even US Dollars), you tip the scale out of your own favor. No matter how good it seems in the short run, you are harming your medium- to long-run economy, potentially drastically and irrecoverably.

Note that this is a Schumpeterian (and Kaldorian) view of trade. Interestingly, L. Randall Wray, one of the founders of MMT, was a student of Minsky, who was a student of Schumpeter. So not only is there the direct lineage of the "Minsky Moment" to MMT, there is also (potentially) almost direct lineage to this view of trade.

Economic Geography

The emphasis on agglomeration effects from increasing returns industry brings us to economic geography. Basically, you want agglomeration of high-tech to occur into your country, not out of your country. You will suffer if it flows out of your country as 1) you will lose high-tech industry to other countries 2) you will be forced to try to buy high-tech products by selling low tech products (or go without), which is always a losing game.

Industrial, manufacturing, and high-technology industries are never at "equilibrium". If they aren't agglomerating into your country, then they are agglomerating out of your country.

At any rate these simple facts both give guidance for immediate policy and provide a powerful lens for viewing the last thousand years of development. The history of colonization and global development is profoundly marked by who had agglomerating, increasing returns industries and those who did not.

An older, related work by myself:

Ballinger, Clint. 2011. "Mercantilism and the Rise of the West: Towards a Geography of Mercantilism." Working paper, available at SSRN or Researchgate.

FURTHER READING

I began my interest in economics from when, in my late teens, I began trying to understand what was meant in the newspapers by the "crisis" of the national debt. I read a great deal in the area most associated with Irving Fisher. Many years later, along somewhat similar lines, I came across the work of Steve Keen.

These works were more focused on what I now understand to be horizontal money. I was missing the vertical component. The light switch was flipped on for me on that side of things by the popular columns in *Forbes* by John T. Harvey. Once I partially "got it" regarding the role and nature of vertical money, I slowly delved deeper into the origins of Modern Monetary Theory and related economics.

This is all apart from my PhD focusing on Economic Geography, which at times overlapped with my understanding of "real" economics - that is, non- equilibrium, real-resource, path-dependent, institutional, historical economics. At any rate, if interested in further reading, I can think of no better place to start than the origins of MMT. Go back to the original works of Warren Mosler, L Randall Wray, Bill Mitchell and Mathew Forstater. And of course the next generation after them, Scott Fullwiler, Pavlina Tcherneva, Stephanie Kelton (Stephanie Bell in early papers) and so on. Many good papers can be found from the Levy Economics Institute of Bard College. It is relatively easy to find these things online now, so I will not attempt further detailed suggestions.

Trade/Economic Geography

Erik Reinert has especially good writing that outlines why understanding increasing and decreasing returns industries is crucial to getting trade "right". This is the one addition I believe MMT needs to integrate to have a fully developed heterodox approach to trade. The Hoeschele paper listed first is an excellent example of how to look empirically at the world through this lens (as well as perhaps my paper on mercantilism listed above, which in part builds on Hoeschele).

Hoeschele, Wolfgang. 2002. The Wealth of Nations at the Turn of the Millennium: A Classification System Based on the International Division of Labor. *Economic Geography* 78(2): 221-244.

Reinert, Erik S. 1994. 'Catching-up from way behind - A Third World perspective on First World history' in Fagerberg, Jan, Bart Verspagen and Nick von Tunzelmann (eds.) *The Dynamics of Technology, Trade, and Growth.* Aldershot: Edward Elgar, pp. 168-197.

Reinert, Erik S. 1995. Competitiveness and its Predecessors - a 500 year Cross- National Perspective. *Structural Change and Economic Dynamics* 6: 23-42. 283

Reinert, Erik S. 1996. 'The Role of Technology in the Creation of Rich Nations and Poor Nations: Underdevelopment in a Schumpeterian System', in *Rich Nations- Poor Nations, The Long Run Perspective.* Aldershot: Edward Elgar, pp. 161-188.

Reinert, Erik S. 1998. 'Raw Materials in the History of

Economic Policy: Or Why List (the Protectionist) and
Cobden (the Free Trader) Both Agreed on Free Trade in
Corn', pp. 275-300 in Gary Cook, ed. *The Economics and
Politics of Free Trade; Freedom and Trade: Volume II*. London:
Routledge, pp. 275-300.

Reinert, Erik S. 2004. "How Rich Nations got Rich: Essays in
the History of Economic Policy." Centre for Development
and the Environment, University of Oslo, Working Paper
no. 2004/01.

The accounting of public spending is carried out in an
archaic and confusing manner. Perhaps the best starting
point are two blog posts on Heteconomist.com by Peter
Cooper:

"Exercising Currency Sovereignty Under Self-Imposed Constraints" (10 December 2014)

http://heteconomist.com/exercising-currency-sovereignty-under-self-imposed-constraints/

"Overt Monetary Financing' in Terms of Simplicity and
Transparency" (2 August 2016)

http://heteconomist.com/overt-monetary-financing-in-terms-of-simplicity-and-transparency/

More in-depth:

Fullwiler, Scott. 2011. "Treasury Debt Operations: An Analysis Integrating Social Fabric Matrix and Social Accounting Matrix Methodologies." SSRN.

Tymoigne, Éric. 2014. "Modern Money Theory and Interrelations between the Treasury and the Central Bank: The Case of the United States" by Levy Economics Institute of Bard College.

L. Randall Wray has an earlier applied explanation that I found useful, especially the last four paragraphs:

Wray, L. Randall. 2001. "Financing state and local government infrastructure investment." Center for Full Employment and Price Stability, University of Missouri - Kansas City, Special Report 01/03.

The best books in textbook form on these topics:

Mitchell, Mitchell, L. Randall Wray, and Martin Watts. 2019. *Macroeconomics*. Macmillan (Red Globe Press)

Godley, Wynne and Marc Lavoie. 2007. *Monetary Economics: An Integrated Approach to Credit, Money, Income, Production, and Wealth*. New York, NY: Palgrave Macmillan.

Tygmoigne, Éric Central Banking, *Asset Prices and Financial Fragility*.

Post by economist John T. Harvey (Texas Christian University, Fort Worth):
"Why Social Security Cannot Go Bankrupt"Apr 8, 2011
https://www.forbes.com/sites/johntharvey/2011/04/08/why-

social-security-cannot-go-bankrupt/#63091e515277

Many of Harvey's other *Forbes* posts are well worth a read.

Additional notes, print edition

Two common reasons given for rejecting MMT are almost opposite in nature. One is that "MMT" somehow allows or encourages spending in a manner that would be inflationary. However, whether in the current system or with any changes, the accounting of spending from a currency issuer is always the same—"spending" is the real resources a democracy decides to use for public purpose; the token system invented by the people to carry this out is unlimited and merely serves an organizational purpose, and cannot "fund" anything whatsoever. Taxes only serve to maintain the functioning of this transfer system.

A different criticism is not that there is too much spending/creation of government money (as above) but that there is *too little*. This comes from critics who (rightfully) worry about the size (and quality) of the private bank-credit (System One) part of the economy.

"Monopoly On Dollars"

The criticism from this angle is that the common mention within MMT of a "monopoly on dollars" (or whatever the tax-credit is: pounds, Australian dollars, złoty etc, depending on the currency issuer) is either false or too small to have the effects that MMT says it does.

Basically, this comes from not understanding that the promises-to-pay that banks make and that serve as "money" for most citizens are just that: just promises and not the actual unit.

The US government does indeed have a monopoly on the

creation of "real" dollars, just like crusoes on the Island (and the UK on pounds, and so on). At the same time, it is true that bank promises-to-pay are used for most immediate transactions an individual will make. The important thing to remember is that the monopoly on "real" dollars is "enough" to allow/cause the system to function in the manner MMT says it does.

Banks have real dollars to settle transactions and to make final settlements on our behalves with the government. This makes the dynamics that MMT outlines occur.

More fundamentally, the government can create the unit-of-account—the tax-credit—at will, allowing the most fundamental fact of sovereignty: it can transfer private resources to the public sphere at will. The money system makes this system a useful market-based process rather than a harsh (and impossibly complex) command process.

The key point is that the monopoly is indeed 100%; the fact that there is a larger system *based on* the dollar (or pound etc) does not mean the system does not work in the way MMT says, the way a monopoly on the dollar (or pound etc) will work.

"97 Percent Of Money Is Bank Credit Money"

Relatedly, the appearance that the government unit monopoly is "minuscule" and seemingly irrelevant in its size is often a reason given by those who believe MMT is in error.

Remember: under existing (and archaic) arrangements, government "money" does not get saved by the private sector as tax-credits. Savers have banks redeem their promises-to-pay for a different government token ("bonds").

So the actual total amount of government money is not

the 3%:97% ratio some highlight. It includes saved "money" which, for example, in the UK, is around 1.7 trillion pounds, and 22 trillion dollars in the United States. The proper comparison of credit-money and government money instruments shows that government money is not at all "insignificant." It is just that people save in government money, whereas bank credit-money is the "lightest" money floating around on top of the system, and thus more visible.

The point is, government "money" and bank-credit "money" are both important in their own way, and again, the "monopoly on money" that MMT discusses does indeed function as they say; the magnitude of bank credit-money, while having genuine detrimental effects if good rules of finance and banking are not followed, in no way undermines the concepts MMT has highlighted as important, and the dynamics they have shown to exist.

The current system that does not allow citizens to directly save and transact in tax-credits, combined with archaic maneuvering of accounts to force the changing of tax-credits into "bonds" both work strongly to make people believe that the government does not have a monopoly on "money" (it has a monopoly on $ r pounds, and this is enough to do what MMT says) and that government "money" is not important (both systems are large; they operate largely on different levels of the economy than each other).

Natural Division Into Two Systems.

As an undergraduate was read a great deal of the highly underrated economic works of Jane Jacobs.

Social capital and similar theories very influential in studies of economic development. In some sense they all boil down to two categories – 1) groups with more or better social capital/trust/ and 2) those without or with less or the wrong kind (amoral familism).

Jacobs, however, goes deeper (in Jacobs, Jane, 1992, *Systems of Survival: A Dialogue on the Moral Foundations of Commerce and Politics*), and shows why there are two basic systems, and why they are intrinsic to society (not just an category social scientists have created) and why they are as they are.

After I started an early version of this book, I realized the obvious similarity. There are two fundamental systems of organizing production (System One and System Two) like Jacobs' two Syndromes.

At first I thought they may be exactly the same, and the works could simply be unified as different "discoveries" of the same aspect of social organization, although there are differences.

However, the "trading" syndrome and the private sector system and the "taking" system" and the public sector system to some extent overlap.

The basic foundations of the public system rely on sovereignty, a monopoly on power. Ultimately the tax-credit system is "taking", although mitigated over the centuries and transformed into a democratically decided taking.

The key insights from Jacobs are useful here though. *Systems of Survival* gives guidance on what 1) kind of rules to make regarding the private system 2) clarification on why trying to force private sector practices on the public sector are a very bad idea. What to some extent seem like negative moral values to our modern ears have a place in public life, and *Systems of Survival* shows why. As I note elsewhere (footnote 152, page 224 of my dissertation):

"Jacobs' typology is more subtle than this table suggests. Jacobs attempts to show that both syndromes are good in the proper context; government plays many legitimate guardian roles, such as defense and police work, anti-trust laws, or sanitation enforcement. The problem comes when the two syndromes mix, as when police or government officials trade their power for wealth, or commercial people use force or deception and fail to innovate, or monopolies lose the commercial morals of thrift and innovation because of lack of competition, and use force to obtain their goals. However, when the guardian aspect of government is larger than it needs to be, the probability of 'syndrome mixing' increases, and a highly guardian society would be similar to other ideas such as amoral familism."

The terminology and more in-depth explanation of Jacobs' "Two Syndromes" and related social capital work can be found in Ballinger, 2008, "Initial Conditions as Exogenous Factors in Spatial Explanation," page 221, "The Two Worlds of Social Capital."

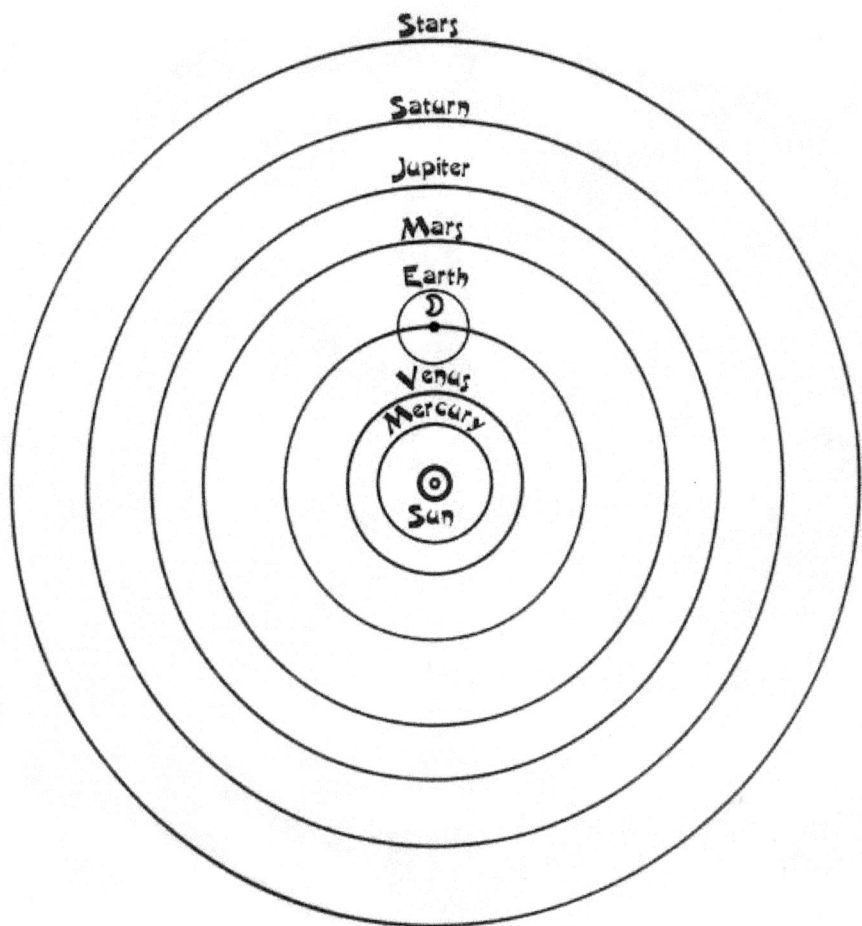

Stars

Saturn

Jupiter

Mars

Earth

☽

Venus

Mercury

☉

Sun

www.ingramcontent.com/pod-product-compliance
Lightning Source LLC
Chambersburg PA
CBHW071434210326
41597CB00020B/3794